Designed for
Google™ earth

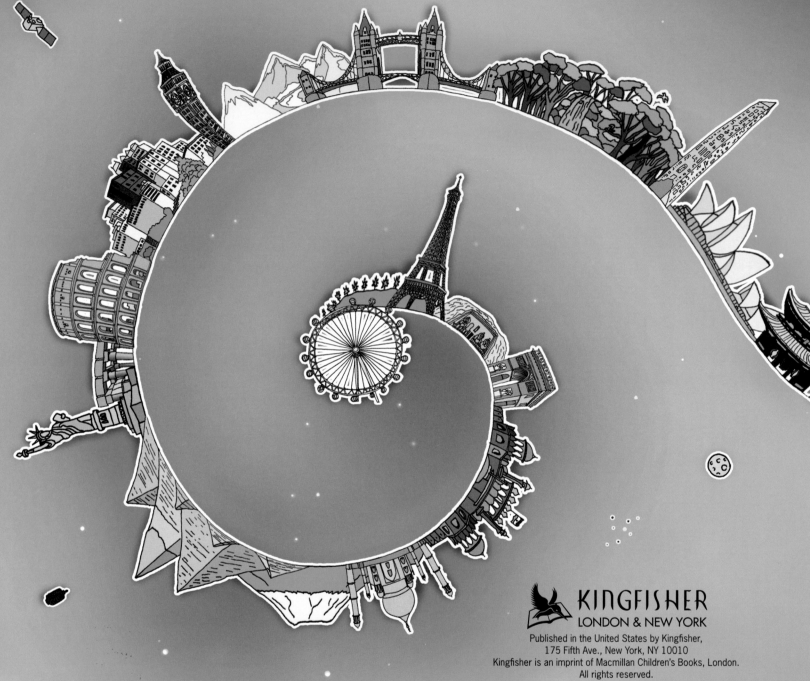

**KINGFISHER**
LONDON & NEW YORK

Published in the United States by Kingfisher,
175 Fifth Ave., New York, NY 10010
Kingfisher is an imprint of Macmillan Children's Books, London.
All rights reserved.

Text, design, and illustration © Carlton Books Limited 2011
Executive Editor: Selina Wood
Art Editors: Laura Templeton, Emily Clarke
Production: Claire Halligan

Distributed in the U.S. by Macmillan,
175 Fifth Ave., New York, NY 10010

Library of Congress Cataloging-in-Publication data has been applied for.
ISBN: 978-0-7534-6721-3

Kingfisher books are available for special promotions
and premiums. For details contact: Special Markets Department,
Macmillan, 175 Fifth Avenue, New York, NY 10010.
For more information, please visit www.kingfisherbooks.com

Printed and bound in Dubai
2 4 6 8 10 9 7 5 3 1

# THE GREAT · GLOBAL · PUZZLE CHALLENGE

with GOOGLE EARTH

Written by
Clive Gifford

Illustrated by
William Ings

KINGFISHER
NEW YORK

## Have you ever wanted to go on a travel adventure around the globe?

Well, set your compass for a great global puzzle challenge— with help from Google Earth! Explore busy cities and awesome landscapes. Navigate your way around the planet and solve brainteasing puzzles to discover your final, top-secret destination!

### Introducing Google Earth

Google Earth is a fantastic mapping program that lets you see close-up images of locations from all over the world on your computer. It is a virtual globe built up from thousands of satellite images of Earth. You can type in addresses, locations, and terrains from all over the world and zoom in to see them close up.

### Getting Google Earth

Google Earth will work on almost all modern personal computers (PCs) and Macs (see the back of the book for more details). Head on to the web at **http://earth.google.com/** or go to **www.google.com**, click on "More" and "even more," and select "Earth." Downloading and installing the Google Earth program is free and takes just a few minutes.

When you run the program, you will see a screen split into a main image window and a navigation panel, which usually lies to the left. The main window is where an image of all or part of Earth is displayed.

### Mouse Controls

By clicking on the main window, you can use your mouse to move the image of Earth. Left click and then drag your mouse to rotate Earth around. If your mouse has a scroll wheel, rolling that forward will help you zoom in closer to Earth's surface. Scrolling back will zoom you further out.

Stonehenge ancient stone circle, England

Zoom in for close-up view

View in 3-

Main window

Navigation panel

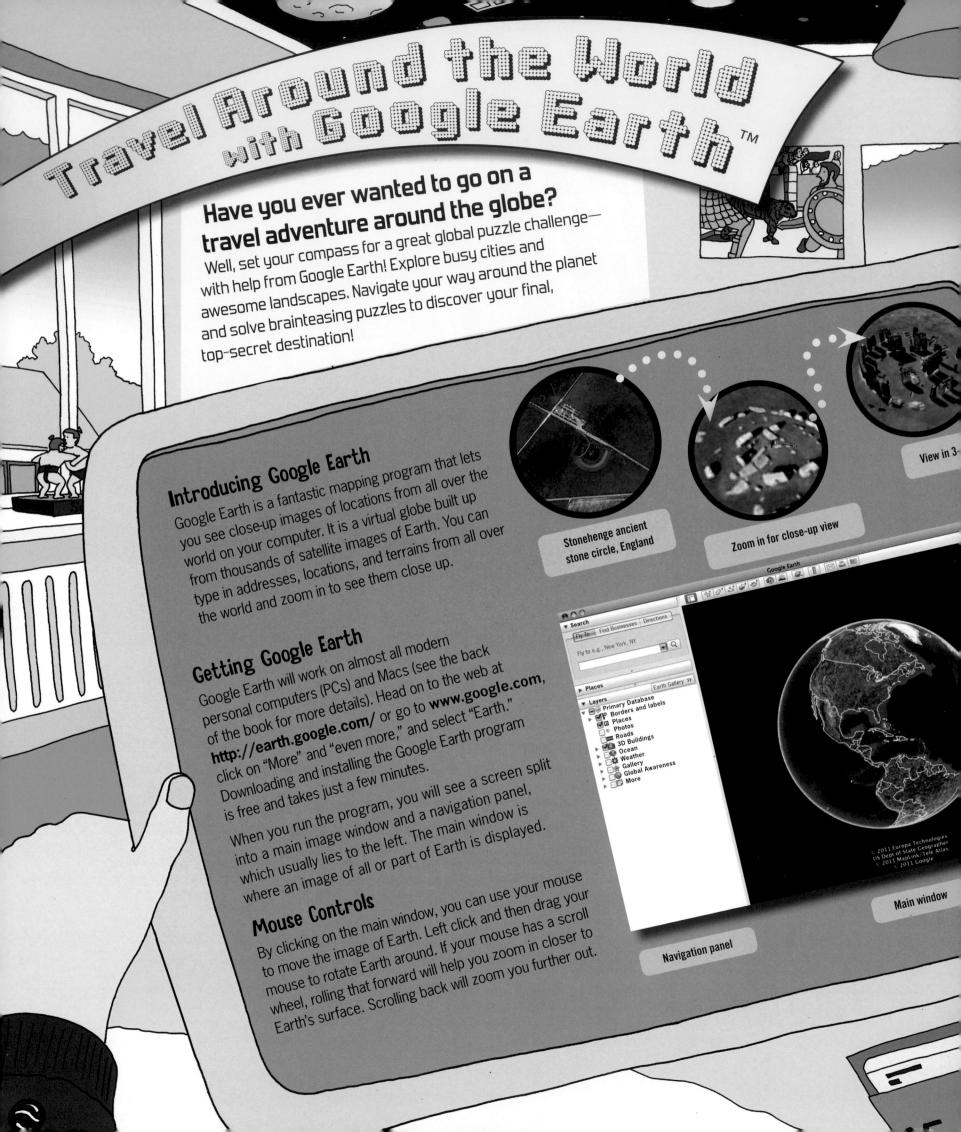

## The "Fly To" Window

In the navigation panel stands a "Search" box that has a tab at the top called "Fly To." Always keep the search box switched onto this. You can click your cursor on the search box and type in a place name. For example, type in the word **Stonehenge** to get to the famous stone circle in England. Press the magnifying-glass icon to start your search.

Many places in Google Earth need to be found by using a long string of numbers and compass points called coordinates. Always be careful to enter the decimal points (the periods) and the correct spaces between numbers. Once you have typed in the coordinates in the "Fly To" box, press the magnifying-glass icon to take you to your location.

To check that you are entering coordinates correctly, try out this test location: **41 53 25.00 N 12 29 32.43 E** It will take you to the Colosseum in Rome, Italy.

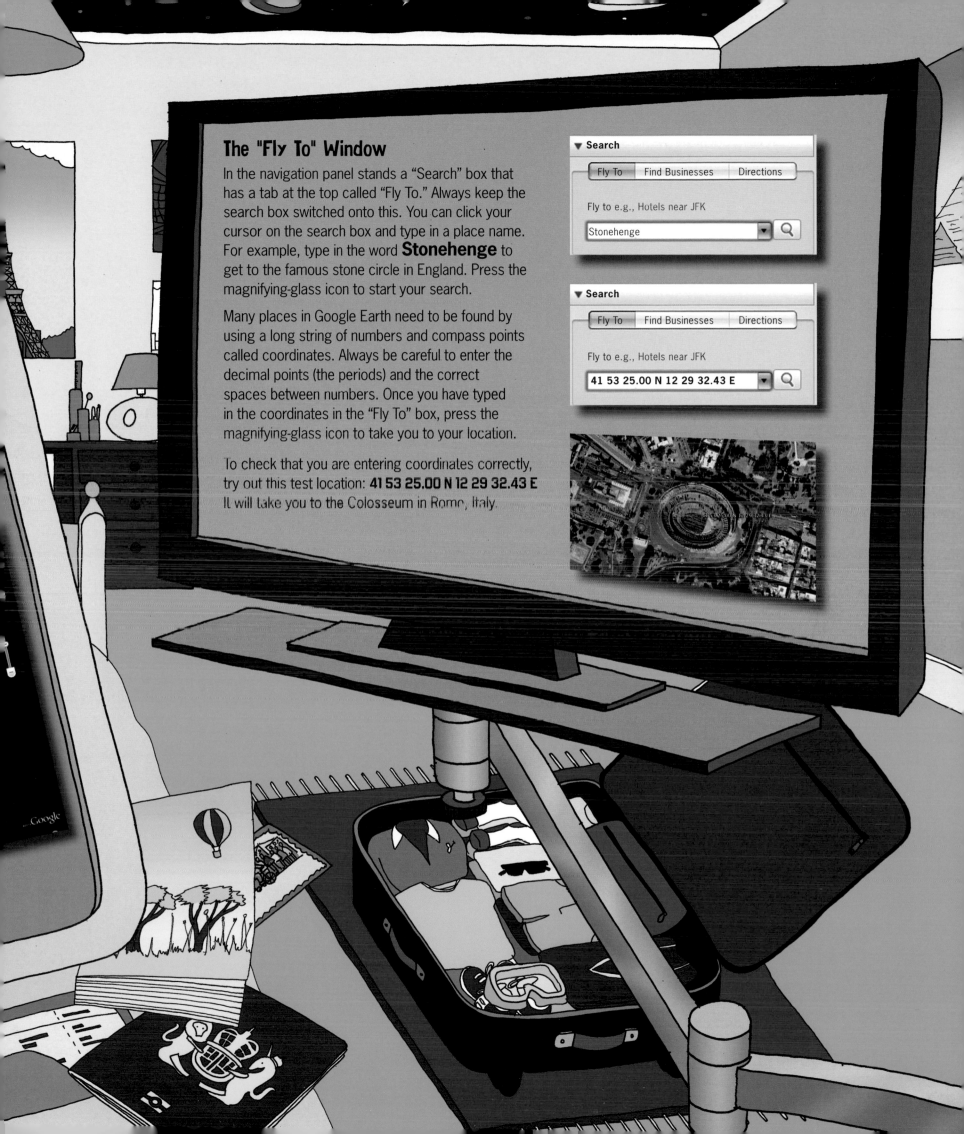

**Google Earth** has many features and controls that you can experiment with. On these pages you can read all about the key controls that you will need to complete your Great Global Puzzle Challenge.

## Layers

In the navigation panel of Google Earth (usually found on the left), there is a section called "Layers." Open that up and there is a long series of boxes that you can click on to check or uncheck. Where a box has a plus or arrow sign beside it, you can click on that to view more boxes. You need only the following boxes checked for this book:

- Borders and Labels
- Places
- 3D Buildings
  (only the "Photorealistic" box, not the "Gray" box or "Trees" box).

▼ Layers                          Earth Gallery

▼ ☐─◇ **Primary Database**
▶ ☑⚐ **Borders and Labels**
▶ ☑▢ **Places**
  ☐▤ Photos
  ☐▭ Roads
▶ ☑▣ **3D Buildings**
▶ ☐🌐 Ocean
▶ ☐✲ Weather
▶ ☐★ Gallery
▶ ☐🌐 Global Awareness
▶ ☐▢ More

## Navigation Controls

Move your mouse over to the top right of the main image window. You should see a pair of circles or wheels and a slider. If these controls cannot be seen, go to the "View" menu at the top, click on "Show Navigation," and select the "Automatically" option.

## Look Joystick

This controls your viewpoint in several ways. You can drag the outer ring and turn it so that your view rotates. Try it out on the Stonehenge location on the previous page and watch the stones rotate around you.

## Move Joystick

This tool allows you to move around Earth in any direction. Click your left mouse button on a direction once to move a short distance or hold the button down to keep moving.

**Zoom!** Click on the **Zoom slider**, which you can drag up to zoom in and drag down to zoom out of a location.

**Tilt! or Getting Low** When you get to a location, the view you are shown is similar to what you would see if you were in a helicopter hovering directly above it. This is called a top-down view. It's great for looking at some things, but to get the most out of 3D buildings or giant mountains, you need to tilt to get low to the ground.

If you zoom really close to the ground using the zoom slider instead of your mouse, Google Earth will tilt automatically. You can also use the up arrow of the Look Joystick. Click on it, hold it down, and watch your viewpoint tilt so that eventually the horizon—where the sky and land appear to meet—can be viewed. You may have to scroll your scene up the screen, but the image from the ground up is well worth it!

Sydney Harbour Bridge, Australia

Top-down view

Tilted view

# Your Puzzle Challenge!

Your mission is to travel the world using Google Earth to explore many fascinating locations. On each double page, you will go to a different destination that you can find on Google Earth. You will be asked to spot certain people, animals, or objects in the illustrations and also to:

● pick up a souvenir

● spot a country's flag or an emblem

● spot a geographical misfit (an object, animal, or person that is in the wrong country or landscape)

● spot a historical misfit (something that's from the wrong historical era)

There will also be a number of puzzles, including a Google Earth search that will reveal a number. As you find each number, write it down either in the spaces below or on a spare piece of paper.

These numbers are crucial because they add up to a complete coordinate to an exciting final destination. Where is it? Ah, that's a secret! At least for now. To start you off, we have filled in the first number—zero—for you. Just 14 more numbers to go. **Good luck!**

**By the way, all of the answers can be found at the back of the book!**

0

# London

51 30 03.16 N
0 07 29.04 W

**Welcome** to your **first** destination! **London** is the capital city of the United Kingdom. It's a huge, bustling place full of historic buildings, such as St. Paul's Cathedral and the Tower of London, and there's plenty to do and see. Many visitors can't resist viewing the city, like we do here, from the giant London Eye wheel standing on the bank of the River Thames . . .

Buckingham Palace

Big Ben

## What can you spot?

The River Thames runs through the heart of the city. Today, you can see boats carrying commuters and tourists and a footrace taking place on its banks. Can you also spot:

- A policeman
- A London taxicab
- Royal Guards on parade?

## VISIT BIG BEN

From the London Eye, cross Westminster Bridge over the River Thames. On the other side is the Palace of Westminster, which is the meeting place of the U.K. parliament. Its tall tower is called Big Ben, after the giant bell inside, which weighs more than 14 tons. Type "Big Ben" into Google Earth to explore the building and tower. How many clock faces does Big Ben have? That number is the second coordinate for your secret final location. Keep it safe!

# Ancient Rome

41 53 25.00 N 12 29 32.43 E

**You've headed back in time** almost 2,000 years to **Rome**, the center of the mighty Roman Empire. Slaves were trained to amuse Roman citizens by taking part in bloodthirsty gladiatorial games. These were battles between gladiators or slaves and wild animals. Listen! You can hear the shouting and cheering!

## SOUVENIR HUNT!

You'll want something to wear at the best event in Rome. High up, it belongs to a gladiator.

## What can you spot?

The Colosseum in Rome was a giant arena where the biggest gladiatorial games took place. There was an amazing atmosphere on days when it was full of 50,000 or more spectators. Inside the Colosseum, can you spot:

- **The Roman emperor** (look for a purple toga)
- **A group of Roman soldiers covered by shields**
- **A Roman vase?**

## Roman numerals

| | | | | |
|---|---|---|---|---|
| = I | | 6 = | VI | |
| = II | | 7 = | VII | |
| = III | | 8 = | VIII | |
| = IV | | 9 = | IX | |
| = V | | 10 = | X | |

## THE FORUM

Type "Roman Forum" into Google Earth to explore the ruins of the Roman Forum in modern-day Rome, Italy. The Forum was a marketplace where Romans shopped and talked politics. Take a look at the many ancient buildings and find the ruins of the Temple of Saturn. Count the number of pillars at that temple and take away three. Add this number to your coordinates for the final destination.

## NUMBER SYSTEM

The Romans had their own number system. It had no symbol for zero, but 0 is the third number of the secret location coordinate, so write it down. And once you have, **try to find the Roman numeral for five in the picture.**

## FIGHTING FAMILIES

Now, it's on to the next destination, the Colosseum as it is today. But before that, you have to solve the following puzzle:

**Spartacus was a famous gladiator. If the son of another gladiator named Rutuba is the father of Spartacus, how are Rutuba and Spartacus related?**

## GLADIATOR SCHOOL

Take a look at the Colosseum on Google Earth. Then type in these coordinates:

**41 53 24.55 N 12 29 41.97 E**
Head to the ruins of the Ludus Magnus, a large gladiator training school. It was linked to the Colosseum by an underground tunnel that took gladiators and caged wild animals into a network of passageways under the floor of the Colosseum's arena.

Lions, ostrich, and rhinoceros were all part of the games at the Colosseum. They were captured from the plains of Africa, which is where you are heading next!

# Tanzania

6 22 8.50 S 34 53 19.76 E

**You've** left Rome for Africa and the plains of **Tanzania**. The plains are home to astonishing animals, including lions, buffalo, rhinoceros, elephants, and wildebeests. These and many other animals gather at watering holes to drink.

## What can you spot?

There are animals everywhere— in the water, hiding in the grass, or ready to sprint. Can you spot:

- A lone cheetah
- A single zebra among the wildebeests
- A hideout where people can watch the animals close up?

## ANIMAL ANAGRAMS

Next, you'll be heading to the highest point in all of Africa. But first of all, try to solve these anagrams to find the names of animals found in Tanzania:

- nilo
- neat help
- lone tape
- choir snore

## TOP OF THE WORLD

**3 04 27.45 S 37 21 30.91 E** Type in these coordinates to go to Africa's highest mountain—Kilimanjaro. On its lower slopes, farmers grow plantains and coffee. At the top, snow and ice cover some of the rocks. The highest point on Kilimanjaro is called Uhuru Peak. Add up the digits that make up the height in feet and subtract 14. The answer is the fifth part of the secret destination coordinates.

**Uhuru Peak**

**Kilimanjaro**

**19,340 ft. (5,895m)**

## NGORONGORO CRATER

**3 11 05.49 S 35 32 42.08 E**

Take a look at the Ngorongoro Crater on Google Earth. Just like Kilimanjaro, Ngorongoro was once a giant volcano. Around two million years ago, it exploded and collapsed in on itself. A large lake formed, which attracts more than 25,000 large animals, including lions, hippos, and brightly colored flamingos.

Your next destination also features a volcano —called Mount Fuji—that overlooks a famous city in Asia—Tokyo. The 12,400-ft. (3,776-m)-high volcano is the highest mountain in Japan. Good luck!

**SOUVENIR HUNT!** Pick up your souvenir carved out of wood by a local craftsman. Clue: it will hide your face.

# Tokyo

35 39 33.86 N 139 42 02.17 E

**Welcome** to Japan's capital city of Tokyo, one of the biggest cities in the world. We are in Shibuya, a busy district popular with shoppers and young people spotting the latest fashions. From Shibuya station, travelers can take a train to connect with the Shinkansen—the bullet train—which carries people all over Japan at speeds of up to 198 mph (320km/h)!

## What can you spot?

Tokyo has a mix of old customs and buildings and striking new fashions and technology. Can you spot:

- **A woman in a kimono**
- **Sumo wrestlers**
- **A red paper lantern?**

**SOUVENIR HUNT!**
Snap up a souvenir from Tokyo. Clue: an animal, it's made of paper and folded up!

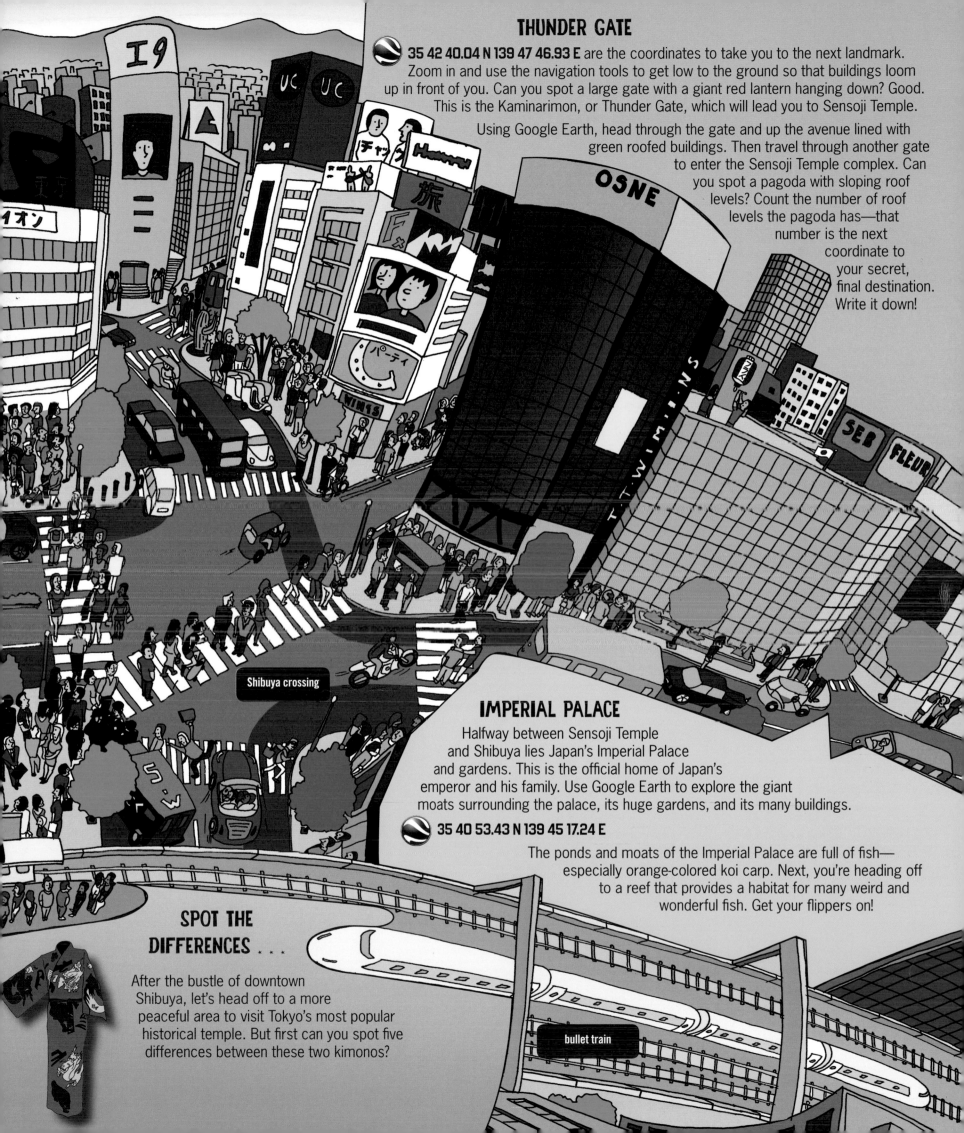

## THUNDER GATE

**35 42 40.04 N 139 47 46.93 E** are the coordinates to take you to the next landmark. Zoom in and use the navigation tools to get low to the ground so that buildings loom up in front of you. Can you spot a large gate with a giant red lantern hanging down? Good. This is the Kaminarimon, or Thunder Gate, which will lead you to Sensoji Temple.

Using Google Earth, head through the gate and up the avenue lined with green roofed buildings. Then travel through another gate to enter the Sensoji Temple complex. Can you spot a pagoda with sloping roof levels? Count the number of roof levels the pagoda has—that number is the next coordinate to your secret, final destination. Write it down!

Shibuya crossing

## IMPERIAL PALACE

Halfway between Sensoji Temple and Shibuya lies Japan's Imperial Palace and gardens. This is the official home of Japan's emperor and his family. Use Google Earth to explore the giant moats surrounding the palace, its huge gardens, and its many buildings.

**35 40 53.43 N 139 45 17.24 E**

The ponds and moats of the Imperial Palace are full of fish—especially orange-colored koi carp. Next, you're heading off to a reef that provides a habitat for many weird and wonderful fish. Get your flippers on!

## SPOT THE DIFFERENCES . . .

After the bustle of downtown Shibuya, let's head off to a more peaceful area to visit Tokyo's most popular historical temple. But first can you spot five differences between these two kimonos?

bullet train

# Great Barrier Reef

16 43 13.49 S
146 12 07.31 E

**SPLISH,** splash, splosh! You've arrived at the **Great Barrier Reef**. Situated off the coast of Australia, it stretches more than 1,240 miles (2,000km) and is made up of the remains of millions of tiny corals. Thousands of visitors dive or go snorkeling to view the reef's wonders up close. You can turn on Google Earth's "Ocean" layer and then click on the icons to view pictures of the reef and underwater life.

## What can you spot?

The reef is home to an incredible diversity of life. There are more than 1,500 types of fish and around 20 reptile species. Among these are sea turtles and giant clams, which can live for more than 100 years. Can you find:

- A giant clam
- A swordfish
- An old shipwreck?

## ISLAND HOPPING

More than 900 islands can be found in or around Australia's Great Barrier Reef coastline. Your next destination is one of those islands. Solve the anagram **MAGIC NET** to type in "............... Island" in Google Earth's search box.

**Clue:** this type of force makes a compass work.

SOUVENIR HUNT!
A wooden toy has been lost in the sea. If you pick it up, you can expect many happy returns!

TROPICAL ISLAND QUIZ
Good job. You've reached a fantastic tropical island. Now use Google Earth to zoom in on the island to answer the questions below. The numbers of the correct answers make up the seventh and eighth numbers for your final, secret destination.

What is the name of the giant bay on the northern shore?
1. North Dolphin Bay   3. Dolphin Cove
2. Coral Bay           4. Horseshoe Bay

Which bay on the island has both a swimming area and a large harbor?
1. Picnic Bay   3. Arcadia Bay
2. Nelly Bay    4. Coral Bay

SYDNEY HARBOUR
33 51 11.41 S 151 12 45.07 E

Type in the coordinates above to visit the large harbour of Australia's biggest city, Sydney. Use the top navigation wheel to get low to the ground and turn to view the 440-ft. (134-m)-high Sydney Harbour Bridge. Nearby is the Sydney Opera House, built in 1973, and its shell-like roof structures. The Sydney Harbour Bridge is the world's tallest single steel arch bridge.

We're continuing to go up as we journey to the highest mountain range in the world.

# Himalayas

27 41 24.49 N 86 44 12.63 E

**FROM** sea level in Australia, you have traveled high into the foothills of the **Himalayas**. This gigantic mountain range stretches across parts of Nepal, India, Pakistan, Bhutan, Tibet, and China. It contains nine of the ten highest mountains in the world! Many visitors start their trip by flying in to the small mountain airport in Lukla, Nepal, more than 10,000 ft. (2,800m) above sea level.

## What can you spot?

You can see hikers and mountaineers on the lower and higher slopes of the mountains. They prepare carefully and take a lot of equipment on their climbing expeditions. Can you spot:

- An oxygen bottle and mask
- A man with two ice axes
- A snow leopard?

## CLIMBING UP . . .

Climb this peak, making camp several times, so that the seven letters spell the name of a famous mountain. You can move straight up or diagonally, but only one letter at a time, and you must move up one level of the letter mountain each time. If you get it right and type that name into Google Earth, you'll be off to your next destination. Start at "E."

## REACH FOR THE TOP

You've been placed on a steep rock wall. Zoom out and reach the top of the world's highest mountain. Explore its different sides and fly along the southern ridge to its neighboring peak, Lhotse. Mount Everest was first successfully climbed in 1953 by Sir Edmund Hillary and Tenzing Norgay. Everest's peak stands 29,029 ft. (8,848m) above sea level. Add these numbers together (2+9+0+2+9) and then add the number 10 to that total. Your final number makes up the next two digits of the coordinates to your secret location.

Have you remembered to look for the flags and the two misfits on each double page? One is historical and one is geographical.

## SOUVENIR HUNT!

Pick up a souvenir from the Himalyas. The clue? You wear it on your head!

## PERFECT PALACE

Enter into Google Earth the coordinates

**29 39 20.78 N 91 07 04.91 E**

to fly northeast of Mount Everest to reach the Tibetan city of Lhasa. See the front gate of a huge 13-story building dedicated to the Buddhist religion.

The Potala Palace has over 1,000 rooms containing 10,000 Buddhist shrines and an incredible 200,000 statues.

One of Tibet's most commonly used gemstones can be found in the palace's first name, Potala. Can you figure it out?

It is four letters long.

With a population of around 300,000, Lhasa is the largest city in Tibet. Your next destination is one of the most populous cities in the United States, with a population estimated at almost nine million—30 times bigger than Lhasa.

```
         T
       S D L
      B E H R
    B Z V R W P
  Z L K Y S E I O J
Q U H A P V X E M Y
T S P U E T K E A J O E
```

40 45 32.44 N
73 59 04.10 W

NEW YORK

Brooklyn Bridge

Empire State Building

Broadway

# Welcome

**to the next destination** on your whistlestop tour of the world. **New York City** is one of the most exciting cities on Earth. Manhattan Island is the heart of the city. There is so much to see and do. Now it's time to explore . . .

## What can you spot?

The **Macy's Thanksgiving Day Parade** is under way in the city. Thanksgiving is traditionally a celebration of the harvest, but this annual parade has become a festive tradition all its own. It is a spectacle of huge balloons heading downtown to the famous Macy's department store. Can you find:

- Cheerleaders
- A spaceman
- Yellow cabs?

**SOUVENIR HUNT!** Pick up your souvenir from New York. The clue? You'd be a mug not to love it!

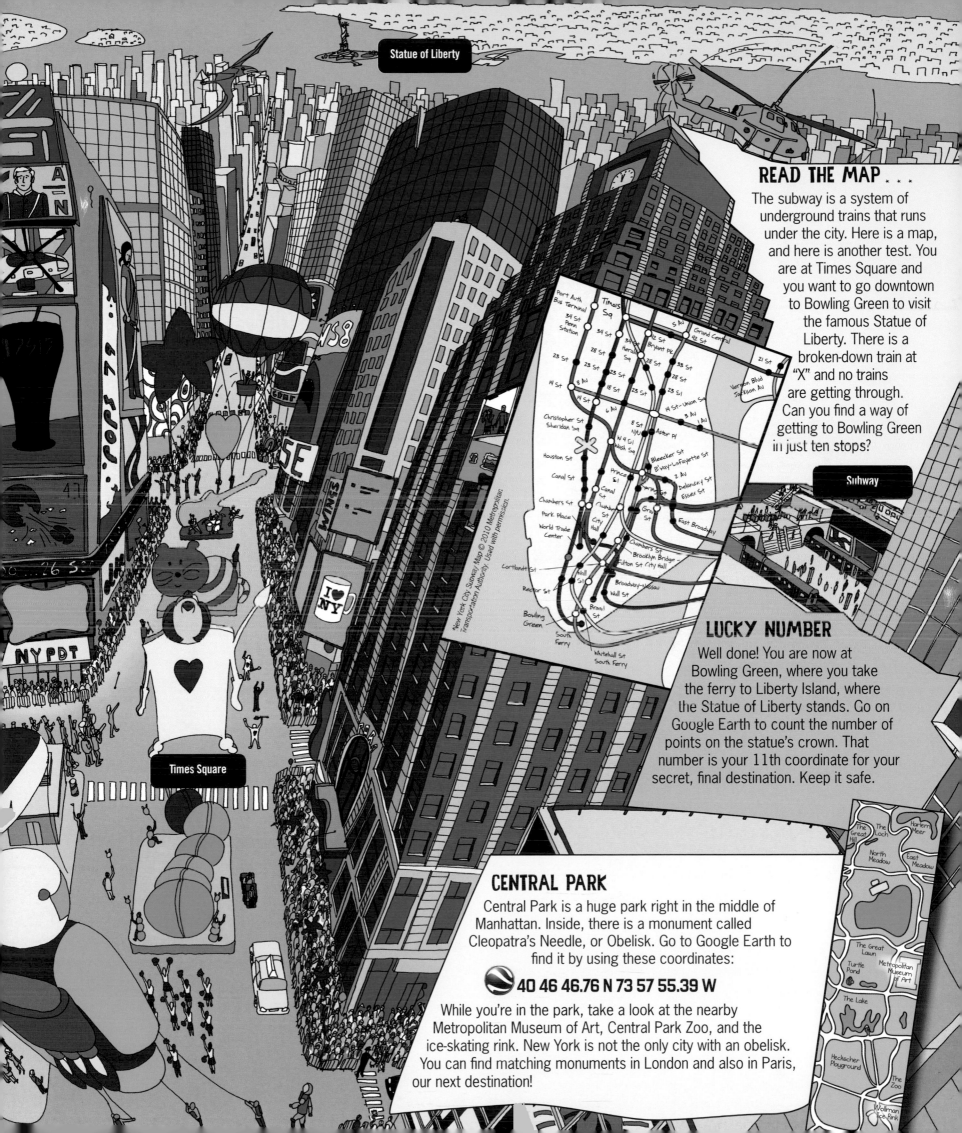

**Statue of Liberty**

## READ THE MAP...

The subway is a system of underground trains that runs under the city. Here is a map, and here is another test. You are at Times Square and you want to go downtown to Bowling Green to visit the famous Statue of Liberty. There is a broken-down train at "X" and no trains are getting through. Can you find a way of getting to Bowling Green in just ten stops?

**Subway**

## LUCKY NUMBER

Well done! You are now at Bowling Green, where you take the ferry to Liberty Island, where the Statue of Liberty stands. Go on Google Earth to count the number of points on the statue's crown. That number is your 11th coordinate for your secret, final destination. Keep it safe.

**Times Square**

## CENTRAL PARK

Central Park is a huge park right in the middle of Manhattan. Inside, there is a monument called Cleopatra's Needle, or Obelisk. Go to Google Earth to find it by using these coordinates:

🌐 **40 46 46.76 N 73 57 55.39 W**

While you're in the park, take a look at the nearby Metropolitan Museum of Art, Central Park Zoo, and the ice-skating rink. New York is not the only city with an obelisk. You can find matching monuments in London and also in Paris, our next destination!

New York City Subway Map © 2010 Metropolitan Transportation Authority. Used with permission.

# Paris

48 51 15.24 N 2 20 12.79 E

**Eiffel Tower**

**Bonjour!** **You are in Paris**—France's capital city and a place of great history, art, and culture. The Seine River flows through the center of the city, dividing it into left and right banks. The Left Bank is famous for its cafés, artists, and booksellers.

## What can you spot?

More people visit France on vacation— 75 million every year— than any other country, and many of those tourists come to Paris. Can you spot:

• A croissant

• An artist with an easel

• A string of onions?

## AVENUE VIEW

Visit the famous Arc de Triomphe on Google Earth. The huge arch sits in the middle of the Place Charles de Gaulle. Count all of the roads or avenues that link up there. Enter that two-digit number into both gaps in the coordinates below. Then type in your coordinates to lead you to your next location:

48 51 28. __ N 2 17 42.__ E

Left Bank

## SOUVENIR HUNT!
You have been "scent" to sniff out a sweet-smelling bargain in a bottle.

René

## TOWERING OVER

The Eiffel Tower, built in 1889, stands more than 985 ft. (300m) high. It took 2.5 million rivets to join all its steel parts together, and it takes 65 tons of paint to repaint the tower every seven years. On Google Earth, count the number of floors the Eiffel Tower has. That number is your 12th secret coordinate. Write it down.

## MUSÉE DU LOUVRE

48 51 43.12 N 2 20 12.04 E are the coordinates that take you to Paris's most famous museum of art. The Louvre is home to many masterpieces, including the *Mona Lisa* by Leonardo da Vinci. Explore its buildings and courtyards and you'll come across some unusual see-through pyramids. The biggest one stands 68 ft. (20.6m) high and is the main entrance into the Louvre.

These modern pyramids are made of steel and glass (the largest Louvre pyramid contains more than 670 panes of glass), but to see some giant, ancient pyramids made of thousands of blocks of stone, just turn the page…

# Ancient Egypt

29 58 38.78 N 31 07 56.34 E

Instead of a flag, can you spot an Eye of Horus?

**You've flown back in time**, more than 4,000 years, to the highly advanced civilization of **ancient Egypt**. Some of ancient Egypt's rulers were buried inside giant stone pyramids. The biggest of all—the Great Pyramid of Khufu—can still be seen at Giza, close to modern-day Egypt's capital city, Cairo. It is built from a staggering 2.3 million blocks of limestone rock, some weighing more than 20 tons—heavier than four adult elephants!

**Pyramid of Menkaure**

## What can you spot?

The Egyptians are hard at work building the third and smallest pyramid at Giza—the Pyramid of Menkaure. The pharaoh, or ruler, is watching from a platform, and there is a religious ceremony taking place outside the second pyramid. There's also a mysterious Sphinx statue featuring a man's face on a lion's body. Can you spot:

- A standing statue of Anubis (a god with a jackal's head)
- A mummy peeping out of the sand
- A scribe drawing on a papyrus scroll?

**SOUVENIR HUNT!** Ancient souvenir Clue: it's a statue in the shape of a feline friend!

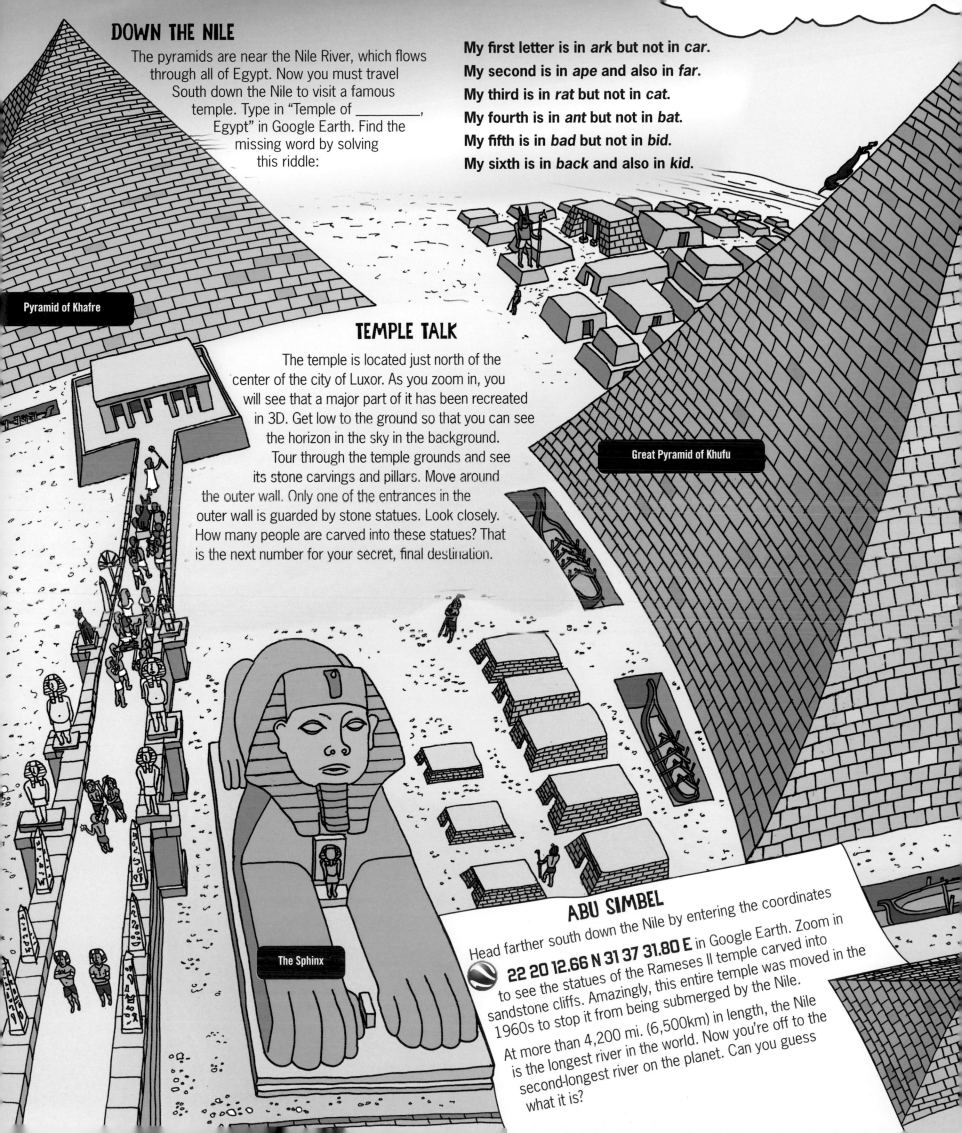

## DOWN THE NILE

The pyramids are near the Nile River, which flows through all of Egypt. Now you must travel South down the Nile to visit a famous temple. Type in "Temple of _____, Egypt" in Google Earth. Find the missing word by solving this riddle:

My first letter is in *ark* but not in *car*.
My second is in *ape* and also in *far*.
My third is in *rat* but not in *cat*.
My fourth is in *ant* but not in *bat*.
My fifth is in *bad* but not in *bid*.
My sixth is in *back* and also in *kid*.

Pyramid of Khafre

## TEMPLE TALK

The temple is located just north of the center of the city of Luxor. As you zoom in, you will see that a major part of it has been recreated in 3D. Get low to the ground so that you can see the horizon in the sky in the background. Tour through the temple grounds and see its stone carvings and pillars. Move around the outer wall. Only one of the entrances in the outer wall is guarded by stone statues. Look closely. How many people are carved into these statues? That is the next number for your secret, final destination.

Great Pyramid of Khufu

The Sphinx

## ABU SIMBEL

Head farther south down the Nile by entering the coordinates 22 20 12.66 N 31 37 31.80 E in Google Earth. Zoom in to see the statues of the Rameses II temple carved into the sandstone cliffs. Amazingly, this entire temple was moved in the 1960s to stop it from being submerged by the Nile. At more than 4,200 mi. (6,500km) in length, the Nile is the longest river in the world. Now you're off to the second-longest river on the planet. Can you guess what it is?

# Amazon Rainforest

2 53 37.00 S 57 44 50.22 W

**From** the dry, sandy lands of Egypt, you've now traveled deep into the dense, wet rainforest of the **Amazon basin**. The rainforest covers a large part of the South American continent. In the middle of it is a huge river known as the Amazon, which includes hundreds of smaller tributary rivers. Above the water level there are millions of trees that form a dense canopy.

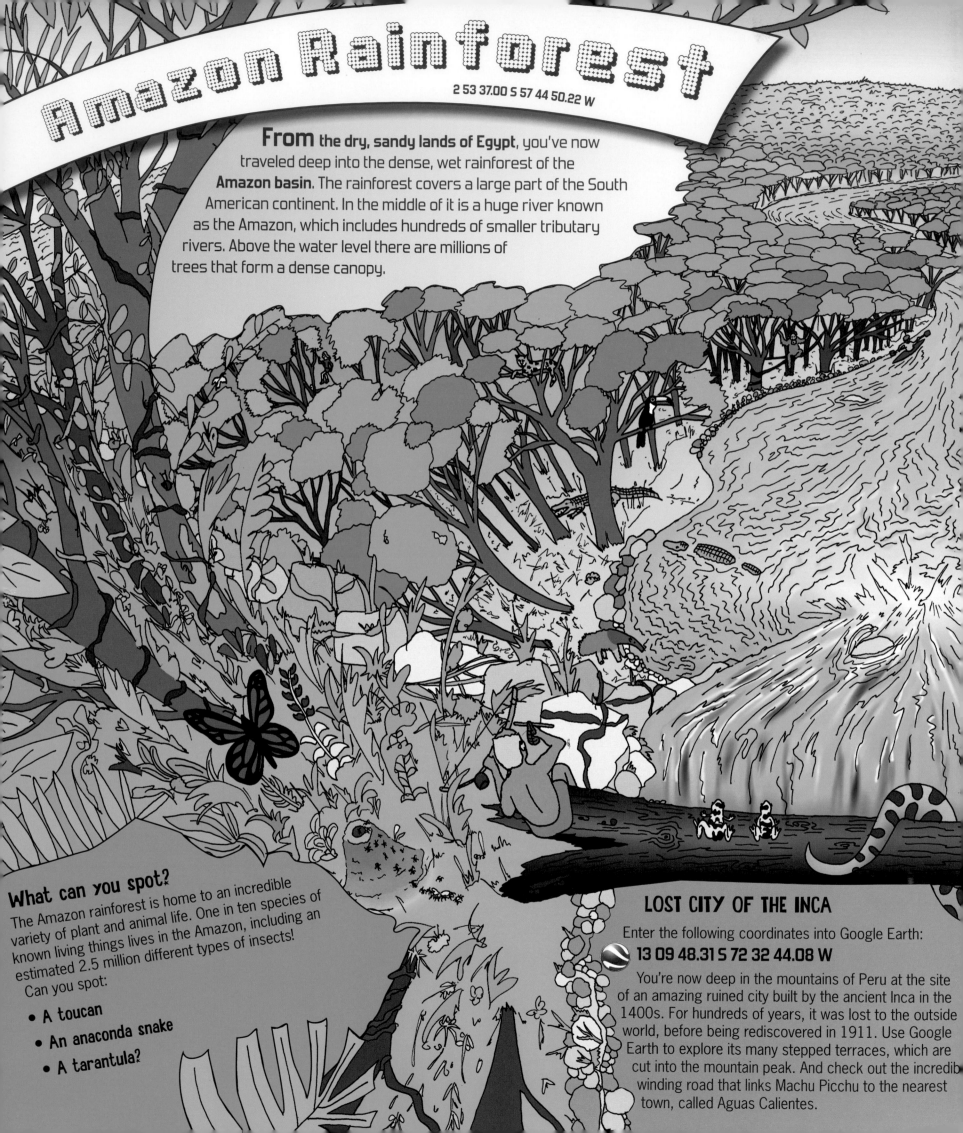

## What can you spot?
The Amazon rainforest is home to an incredible variety of plant and animal life. One in ten species of known living things lives in the Amazon, including an estimated 2.5 million different types of insects!
Can you spot:

- A toucan
- An anaconda snake
- A tarantula?

## LOST CITY OF THE INCA

Enter the following coordinates into Google Earth:
### 13 09 48.31 S 72 32 44.08 W

You're now deep in the mountains of Peru at the site of an amazing ruined city built by the ancient Inca in the 1400s. For hundreds of years, it was lost to the outside world, before being rediscovered in 1911. Use Google Earth to explore its many stepped terraces, which are cut into the mountain peak. And check out the incredible winding road that links Machu Picchu to the nearest town, called Aguas Calientes.

**HOW MANY DIFFERENCES** can you spot between these two pictures of parts of Machu Picchu? That number is the next part of the coordinates for your secret, final destination, so write it down.

**SOUVENIR HUNT!** Pick up your Amazon Souvenir. Clue: Someone is playing it!

## SPORTS STADIUM

Your next Google Earth search is a sporty one, so type in the following coordinates to get moving:

**22 54 43.96 S 43 13 48.69 W**

The Maracanã in the Brazilian city of Rio de Janeiro is a soccer stadium. At the 1950 World Cup, an incredible 199,000 people crammed into the arena to watch the final game. The Maracanã will host more international games when the World Cup returns to Brazil in 2014 and the Olympic Games are held in Rio in 2016.

Your next location is a city in Asia that hosted the 2010 Commonwealth Games featuring thousands of athletes from more than 70 countries.

# New Delhi

28 37 58.00 N 77 13 11.00 E

**You've touched down in India**, home to more than one billion people. Its capital is **New Delhi**, a colorful, thriving city full of monuments, markets, bazaars, and many, many people! Listen, you can hear the hustle and bustle!

## What can you spot?

New Delhi has a population of almost 12 million people. There's so much to see here, including busy streets with rickshaws tooting and bazaars where everything from spices to saris, books to PCs, are bought, sold, and traded. Take a good look around and see if you can find:

- A sacred cow

- A snake charmer

- A Ganesha (Hindu elephant god) shrine?

## AGRA

Head down the Yamuna River to the historic city of Agra, which lies 105 mi. (170km) south of Delhi. Enter the following coordinates into Google Earth: **27 10 47.21 N 78 01 15.87 E** to visit and explore the city's famous Red Fort, which once contained as many as 500 buildings inside its stout, 65-ft. (20-m) high walls.

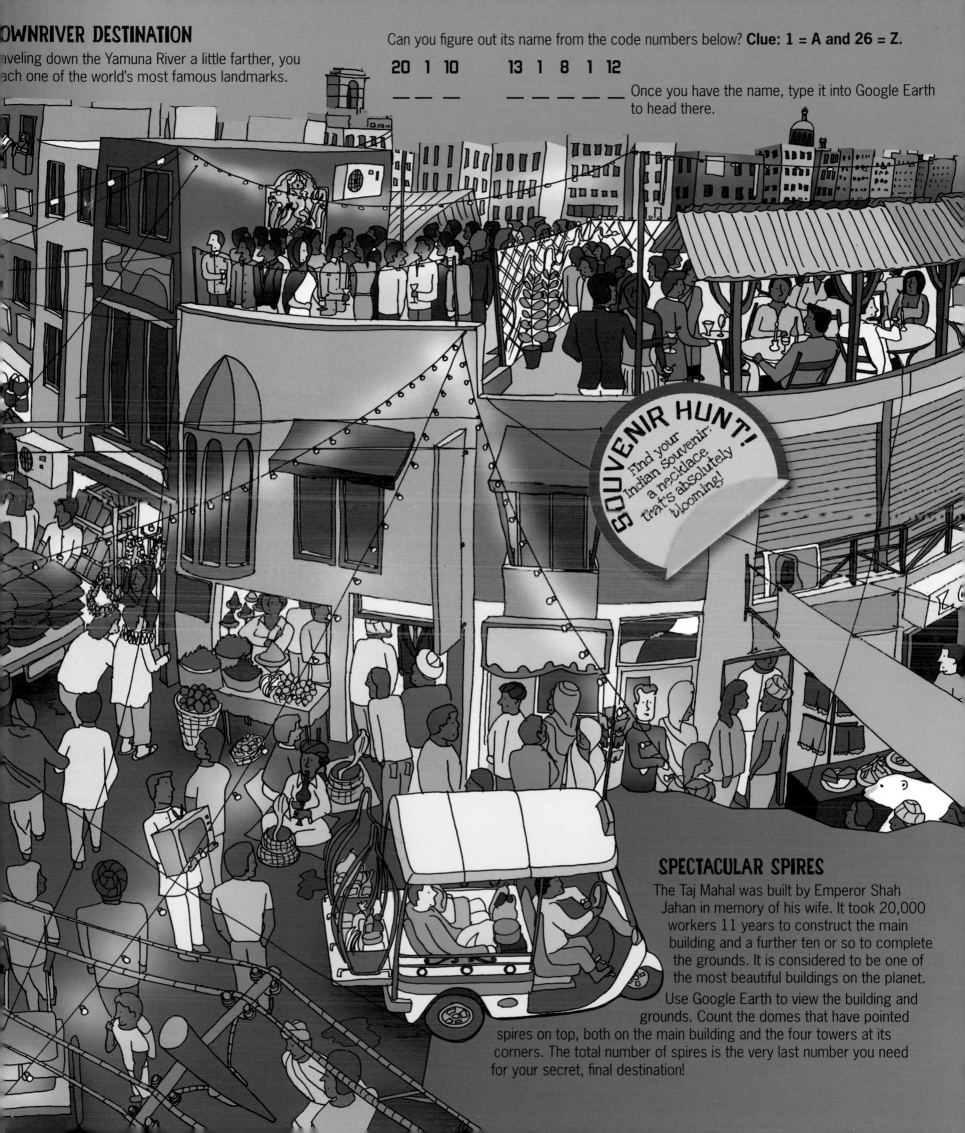

# OWNRIVER DESTINATION

aveling down the Yamuna River a little farther, you
ach one of the world's most famous landmarks.

Can you figure out its name from the code numbers below? **Clue: 1 = A and 26 = Z.**

20 1 10    13 1 8 1 12

_ _ _   _ _ _ _ _    Once you have the name, type it into Google Earth
to head there.

## SOUVENIR HUNT!

Find your Indian souvenir: a necklace that's absolutely blooming!

## SPECTACULAR SPIRES

The Taj Mahal was built by Emperor Shah Jahan in memory of his wife. It took 20,000 workers 11 years to construct the main building and a further ten or so to complete the grounds. It is considered to be one of the most beautiful buildings on the planet.

Use Google Earth to view the building and grounds. Count the domes that have pointed spires on top, both on the main building and the four towers at its corners. The total number of spires is the very last number you need for your secret, final destination!

# Out of This World!

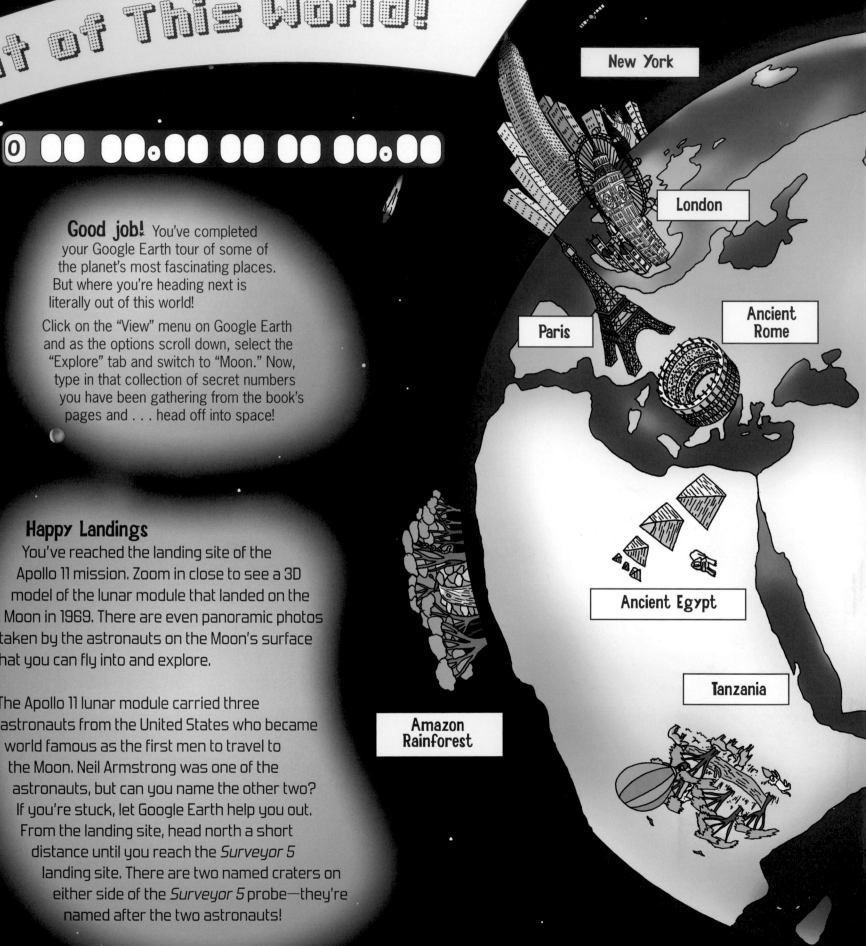

**0 ⬜⬜ ⬜⬜.⬜⬜ ⬜⬜ ⬜⬜ ⬜⬜.⬜⬜**

**Good job!** You've completed your Google Earth tour of some of the planet's most fascinating places. But where you're heading next is literally out of this world!

Click on the "View" menu on Google Earth and as the options scroll down, select the "Explore" tab and switch to "Moon." Now, type in that collection of secret numbers you have been gathering from the book's pages and . . . head off into space!

## Happy Landings

You've reached the landing site of the Apollo 11 mission. Zoom in close to see a 3D model of the lunar module that landed on the Moon in 1969. There are even panoramic photos taken by the astronauts on the Moon's surface that you can fly into and explore.

The Apollo 11 lunar module carried three astronauts from the United States who became world famous as the first men to travel to the Moon. Neil Armstrong was one of the astronauts, but can you name the other two? If you're stuck, let Google Earth help you out. From the landing site, head north a short distance until you reach the *Surveyor 5* landing site. There are two named craters on either side of the *Surveyor 5* probe—they're named after the two astronauts!

New York

London

Paris

Ancient Rome

Ancient Egypt

Tanzania

Amazon Rainforest

Tokyo

Himalayas

New Delhi

Great Barrier
Reef

## The Red Planet

Now, why not head off farther into the solar system and visit Mars? Pull down Google Earth's "View" menu, select "Explore," and click on "Mars." Then, type in the following code words to see interesting locations on the Red Planet:

Type in **Viking I** to view the landing site around the first robot to land safely on and explore Mars.

Type in **Olympus Mons** to view the largest mountain on Mars. It stands an incredible 89,000 ft. (27,000m) above the Martian surface. What a whopper!

Type in **MER Spirit** to visit the landing site and route that the mobile *Spirit* robot took around part of the Red Planet.

## Other Galaxies

Switch to Google Sky by selecting "Sky" from the "Explore" tab on the "View" menu. This gives you a view of the night sky and allows you to travel far past Mars to explore deep space.

Type in **Rigel** in the search box to head off to one of the brightest stars in the sky. Rigel is 35 times bigger than the Sun and shines very brightly. It can be seen clearly in the night sky yet lies more than 700 light years away from Earth.

Type in **M31** to head off to the largest galaxy in the Local Cluster. The Andromeda Galaxy is an eye-watering 2.5 million light years away from Earth and is packed full of stars. Astronomers estimate that the galaxy contains about a trillion stars—that's even more than our own galaxy!

# Puzzle answers

 **London**

Big Ben has **4** clock faces.

The ninth bridge is *Tower Bridge*.

Geographical misfit—*Leaning Tower of Pisa*

Historical misfit—*galleon on the river*

Souvenir—*umbrella (on the London Eye)*

The flag is *on top of Buckingham Palace.*

 **Ancient Rome**

The figure calculated from the Temple of Saturn pillars is **5**.

Geographical misfit—*kangaroo*

Historical misfit—*soccer player in arena*

Souvenir—*gladiator's helmet, top left in Colosseum*

The flag is *by the stairs above the emperor.*

Roman numeral V is *to the right of the soldiers.*

Spartacus is *Rutuba's grandson.*

 **Tanzania**

The figure calculated from Kilimanjaro sign is **3**.

Geographical misfit—*skier*

Historical misfit—*Tyrannosaurus rex*

Souvenir—*wooden mask*

Anagrams—*lion, antelope, elephant, rhinoceros*

The flag is *on the boat.*

 **Tokyo**

The pagoda has **5** roof levels.

Geographical misfit—*cactus*

Historical misfit—*samurai warrior on soccer field*

Souvenir—*origami bird*

Number of differences in the picture—5

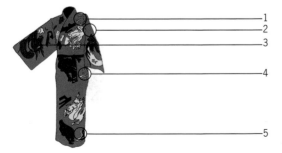

1
2
3

4

5

The flag is *by the buildings on the right.*

 **Great Barrier Reef**

Anagram—*Magnetic Island*

Answers to multiple choice questions—**4** and **2**

Geographical misfit—*rabbit under water*

Historical misfit—*old-fashioned telephone*

Souvenir—*boomerang*

The flag is *on the shipwrecked boat.*

 **Himalayas**

The letter mountain spells "Everest."

The Everest peak puzzle makes **3** and **2**.

The gemstone is *opal.*

Geographical misfit—*sunbather*

Historical misfit—*old-fashioned bicycle*

Souvenir—*Tibetan woolen hat*

The flag is *in the bottom left corner.*

 **New York**

The Statue of Liberty has **7** points on its crown.

*Subway journey—take the yellow line and change at 34 St., then the orange line for three stops, next the blue line for four stops, and finally the green line for two stops.*

Geographical misfit—*igloo*

Historical misfit—*Pterodactyl*

Souvenir—*"I love NY" mug*

The flag is *in the center, above the yellow balloon.*

**▮▮** **Paris**

Number of roads at Arc de Triomphe—12

Next location—*Eiffel Tower*

The Eiffel Tower has **3** floors.

Geographical misfit—*giraffe*

Historical misfit—*chariot and horse*

Souvenir—*perfume*

The flag is *on the car.*

 **Ancient Egypt**

Answer to riddle—*Temple of Karnak*

Karnak has **4** people carved in stone.

Geographical misfit—*penguin*

Historical misfit—*airplane*

Souvenir—*statue of the cat goddess Bastet*

The Eye of Horus is *on one of the large blocks of stone.*

 **Amazon Rainforest**

Number differences in the pictures—**6**

1
2
3
4
5
6

Geographical misfit—*traffic light*

Historical misfit—*record player*

Souvenir—*berimbau, a traditional Brazilian musical instrument*

The flag is *on the moored boat.*

 **New Delhi**

The downriver destination is the *Taj Mahal.*

The Taj Mahal has **9** domes with spires.

Geographical misfit—*polar bear*

Historical misfit—*caveman*

Souvenir—*flower garlands*

The flag is *in a window at the top of the page.*

**Out of This World**

The final coordinates are:

**0 40 53.54 23 27 34.69**

The two astronauts are *"Buzz" Aldrin* and *Michael Collins.*

---

## Computer requirements for running Google Earth

**PC systems**

Operating system: Windows 2000, Windows XP, Windows Vista, or Windows 7

CPU: Pentium III, 500Mhz

System memory (RAM): 256MB

Hard disk: 400MB free space

Network speed: 128 kbits/sec

Graphics card: 3D-capable with 16MB of VRAM

Screen: 1024 x 768, "16-bit high color"—DirectX 9 (to run in Direct X mode)

**Mac systems**

Operating system: Mac OS X 10.4.0 or later

CPU: 1 GHz

System memory (RAM): 256MB

Hard disk: 400MB free space

Network speed: 128 kbits/sec

Graphics card: 3D-capable with 16MB of VRAM

Screen: 1024 x 768, "Thousands of Colors"